Lyn,

a pleasure to have
you in my life —

enjoy my journey

of Poems —

with aloha,

Sue

"It is better to travel well than to arrive"

~ *Buddha*

Dandelion

A collection of poems for family and friends

Sue Savill Lucas

Dandelion

A collection of poems for family and friends
Sue Savill Lucas

ISBN-13:978-1985859487
ISBN-10:1985859483

Published by Dandelion Publishing
Turtle Bay, Hawaii, USA

Designed and produced by Angela Treat Lyon
AngelaTreatLyonBOOKS.com

Dedication

Dandelion is dedicated to
the late Lawrence Hall Dawson,
friend, writer, and mentor.

Acknowledgements

I would like to acknowledge my teachers, mentors, and speakers of higher consciousness who have contributed to my personal growth.

Lawrence Hall Dawson to whom this book is dedicated; Rev. Sky St. John, Rev. Richard Levy, Rev. Lisa Davis, Dave Druz (facilitator of the North Shore Meditation Group), Mata Amritanandamayi (Ammachi), Parmahansa Yogananda, Kriyanda, Chidvilasananda (Gurumayi), Ram Dass, Mother Meera, His Holiness, the Dalai Lama, Louise Hay, Wayne Dyer, Terry McBride, Deepak Chopra, Gary Zukav, Rev. Richard Rogers, Jeanne Morris ... and many many more.

Not to mention the enormous support of my husband, Bob, and my dear friends from all over the world who have encouraged me to put these poems into a book.

And a big thank you to Angela Treat Lyon for her huge help designing and producing *Dandelion*.

Introduction

Sue Savill Lucas is originally from Norwich, England and has been writing poems for several decades.

Sue has been influenced by her worldwide travels and the many friends and teachers she has encountered on her journey.

It is these friends who urged her to put all her poems into a book, so it is therefore a very personal collection.

Why "Dandelion"? Dandy was a childhood name; and is symbolic of the cycles of life. Dandelion originated from Medieval Latin "dens leonis" (lion's tooth), and later, the French "dent de lion" because of the jagged shape of the leaves.

"As children," Sue says, "we enjoyed the "dandelion clock." We would "tell time" by blowing the white seeds: the number of puffs required to blow them all off supposedly being the number of the hour."

Dandelion is both an excellent food, tea and medicine.

Sue Savill Lucas

Table of Contents

Dandelion

A collection of poems for family and friends

Naranja

Bright spark, fiery sphere like the sun
or fused with pink when day is done.
A colour of vibrance, shock and cheer
of pumpkins, tangerines, it's loud and clear.
Of burning hearths and rugs on winter nights,
of marmalade and   juice and children's kites.
Balloons and   flags,
both full and   bold,
concentrates   the many
petalled   marigold.

A signal   between the
red   and green
a glow of light   at night it's seen.
Sequential victim   of a glaring light
warm and helpful in the night.

It flies, it glows and does return
relinquished, smouldering in the urn.
Spinning, radiating in your shroud
no wonder ORANGE you are proud.

Miami, October 1975

1

John / Juan

John moved to California where begins our tale
from middle-class suburbia, Scottsdale.
He drove his Volkswagen here overland
for a view of the ocean, instead of sand.
He was tired of the desert, cacti and heat
and wanted more freaky people to meet.

He worked for a company that sold real estate
very conscientiously and never was late.
He looked very conservative in his suits and ties
but felt more at home in a pair of levis.

He's a Scorpio, but you never could tell
not even after knowing him well.
His sting I've never seen him use
or get angry and his temper lose.
He's kind and patient and will help you out
and calm you down and never shout.

In cultivating his mind, he turned to Spanish
even though sometimes the words would vanish.
He says he finds English hard enough
and another language really tough!

When working he was organized in every way
and had a schedule to keep each day.

Dandelion

Now unemployed, his views have changed
I like him better, not so arranged.
He still drinks water mixed with Scotch
but no longer wears a watch.
He's more relaxed and likes it too
enjoying the things he wants to do.

Now he's leaving his apartment for sure
and putting his things in a locker to store.
He's planning a trip and may never return
to distant places, an experience to learn.
To cities he's only read of in books
of people and cultures, their smells and their looks.
It's something he knows that he wants to do
a change in lifestyle and an education too.

He liked finance games, even as a boy
and playing the stock market is like a toy
except when you lose, you can no longer play
as John quickly found out one day.

He's always investing in something or other
usually unknown to even his mother.
But over his losses, he's never seen moping
because like a game, he keeps on hoping
that all his investments he won't regret
on making some money, his mind is set.

He'll like the diversity of different places
and foreign tongues and alien races
which many Americans seem to skip
and substitute a bigger tip
for a handshake or simple smile
that stays with people for a while.

He'll like the warmth of a Latin lover
and will also then discover
they treat you like the only one
are affectionate and lots of fun.
The cool, calm collected blondes of Sweden
to the American man, a garden of Eden.
They are very free and easy to know
but can be icy, like the snow.

He'll have to watch his money with care
as things are more expensive there.
He can't wait to set off and fill his mind
with a cultural background of mankind.

Los Angeles, California 1970s

Jackie & Russ

At UCLA in the hustle and bustle
starts the true story of Jackie and Russell.
He from a family that traveled afar
from the shores of Tripoli to the Grand Bazaar.
In Istanbul where east and west meet
city of mosques where you wash your feet,
exotic spices fill the air
where baklava is the Turkish fare.
Tea is drunk and tastes so fine
and people talk to pass the time.
One has to bargain in order to stay
and buying one thing may take a whole day.

Once in a while on a fancy whim
a hint of the East is still in him.
Its logic, mystique and unpredictable ways
mixes with reality of weeks and days.

A Royal subject, for what it's worth
London was his place of birth.
A country of rain and fields of flowers
of pubs and puddles, castles and towers.

To the islands of music and life in San Juan
of dancing and eating, those days are gone.
Of tropical fruits and balmy nights
crystal clear water and sparkling lights.

To Africa, Morocco, safaris and sand
where one takes a camel overland

To Canada and winters of blizzards of snow
across continents the family did go.
Finally now in California to stay
near Hollywood, the beaches and...UCLA!

A writer at heart and a talented man
he writes and he draws whenever he can.
To the strange and bizarre he will quite often turn
and there's always something more intriguing to learn.

He will fascinate you with his sensitive touch
but has the ability to annoy you just as much.
He's vague and abstract in his mind and his view
of people and places and things sometimes too.
He can't understand the materialistic throngs
because it's for something much deeper he longs.
He detests peroxide blondes and Hollywood stars
and the Palm Springs set and American cars.

He's honest and may tell you his mind
if you ask his opinion, the truth you will find.
There's not many like him, he's a breed quite apart
and to have as a friend, he'll give you his heart.
Jackie is basic and vibrant and fun,
she talks and laughs like a ray of the sun
and brings to his life a variety of pace
which brings him to earth from outer space.
She has many cousins, several I've met
but so many more, whom I've to see yet.
Her family is large and scattered around
although most on the U.S. west coast are found.

Dandelion

At a computer company she wrote the news
and handled the advertising, giving her views.
Typing she does, but it's not truly her bag
like me, we agree, it's really a drag!

The days of long lunch hours and sitting outside
too numerous to mention the restaurants we tried.
On the pier near the ocean we ate lots of shrimp
even on crutches, I managed to limp.

The sophistication of the well known "Bellevue,"
to the local Deli where we had to queue
from Chinese, Italian to bagels and lox
always at lunchtime were Jaffe and Cox.

A fan of the pickle, especially the dill
to the Viking smorgasbord, we had our fill.
To Buffalo Chips, where the hamburgers are jumbo
to the days of clam chowder and chicken gumbo.
Then we had such amazing luck
to discover the Feed Bag for under a buck!

Within the company she did flourish and grow
and was sent to New York to cover a show,
with the executive men we all know about
she returned to L.A. completely worn out!

One day after work her old car was not there
to the local police station Jackie went in despair
to give a report and relevant detail
they said they'd look out - but quite often fail!

Jackie, not encouraged left with a shrug
but the insurance paid off and she bought a new "Bug".
it's shiny and yellow and a roof for the sun
and learning to shift was novel and fun.

Just about the same time her job came to an end
but was beginning to drive her round the bend.
So not too upset it was to the welfare line
to collect unemployment for a short time
so she thought, but alas still no job she's found
but enjoys the freedom and buzzes around
from free-lancing projects when money is tight
but which cannot substitute for wanting to write.
She's still searching for a job to come her way
one that she'll like with rewarding pay.

They hope in the Spring to go over to Spain
as the smog of L.A may drive them insane.
To relax on the beaches and swim and to write
and dine on paella where they just might
hear serenades of guitars to a haunting tune
of flamenco rhythms by the light of the moon.

In Espana they call her "La Luna"
and maybe they'll leave even sooner
if Russ's Dad wins the Pools
then to stay they'd be fools.
Where people are friendly and time does not matter
and Jackie will slim and Russ will get fatter.

Dandelion

The spirit of adventure is calling them there
and it's only a matter of saving the fare.
Then it's a trip across the Atlantic
where life is slower and the pace is less frantic.
They enjoy good wine and come often to dinner
(even though Jackie is looking much thinner)
the theatre, music, people and art
I do hope they never part!

Los Angeles, California, 1970s

Baja Train

Fields full with corn, straight and proud
each an individual and yet in a crowd.
Where wealth and hunger are near at hand.
To make tortillas, fresh and hot
Mexican families eat a lot.

Past Tequila where the manguey cactus grows
in lush green fields in small neat rows.
The sellers there all climb aboard
with bottles of their golden hoard.
Enough to make a man insane
as tequila breath permeates the train.

Through countryside whose beauty is a sight
fresh and green and bathed in light.
Through hills and valleys with wild orange flowers
a pleasant sight to fill the hours.

Tacos of pollo fresh and hot,
sabroso as snacks, they hit the spot.
Corn with limon, sprinkled with sauce
consumed as the train continues its course.
Delicious tamales hot and sweet
or picante, spicy filled with meat.

Baja, Mexico, early 1970s

Bonnie de la Burrito

She dashes around from appointment to meeting
from morning till night, never stopping for eating.
She leaps in her car and drives from hill to vale
and returns at night to rural Prunedale.

She has the ability to reassure and pace
but left New York to escape the rat race.
She hardly expected to find it out west
but due to the climate, it suits her best.

Tired of paying high rents, she thought she'd invest
and quickly her versatility was put to the test.
She is now a plumber, a gardener, and has learnt how to tile
although swears she will not try it again for a while.

Her bathroom she has completely re-done
to save $200 would have been the sum.
The only help she was given by men
was putting the window in, credit goes to Ken.
Apart from that detail she has done it alone
most would not attempt but merely just moan!

California, Early 1970s

Who Is Hugh

Hugh is a student at U.C.L.A
who studies and also works part of the day
He was studying French but now it's German
although he's prefer to paint like Firmin.

He is young, inexperienced, but eager to learn
and getting good grades is his main concern.
His face is boyish and he loves to munch
after working an hour he must eat his lunch.

Hugh is young, naive with charm
can get uptight but too can be calm.
He longs to see world famous art
and how today it has played its part.

From Renaissance painters of the Italian school
to Modern French, he stops to drool
over a Cezanne, Pissarro, a Renoir or two
and German Expressionists, alas too few.

His taste is expensive, basic and simple
and while showing Munters, he grins with a dimple.
As of German Expressionists he is the most fond
especially the one of the sleeping blonde.

He gingerly gets out paintings and looks
at rare originals seen only in books
by Kandinsky, Jawlensky, Schiele and Pechstein
these paintings are ageless and priceless with time.

Dandelion

Their beauty to see, an investment for many
who are willing to spend the well earned penny.
One day he dreams of owning an original or two
along with a sculpture and a tapestry in blue.

He's intent on learning so many things
and experiencing life and having some flings.
For the first time he's having to cook
and finds that all learning is not in a book.
He longs to travel to distant places
to see the world's wonders and myriad races.

He dreams of Paris, city of the Seine,
to walk in the streets where geniuses came.
The Louvre, Montmartre and just the street scene
of a city that was and is an artist's dream.

Her cafés, boulevards and Parisian flavour
is something everyone simply must savour.
The chic women, night clubs, so typically French,
yet a simple "dejeuner" on a park bench
of a crusty baguette, paté and wine
the French make this snack absolutely divine.

This is the style when one is in France
to wine and dine, enjoy life and dance.
There's a magic in Paris - the city of light
inspiring authors as Hemingway great novels to write.
Her beauty and charm have been written of before
so Hugh must see for himself and not on a tour.

This city is one where time must be given
in walking the streets where artists are driven
seeking a romantic but always so real
picture to paint that no-one can steal.

He thinks of Europe he will become fond
and aspires of becoming "un homme du monde."
To talk with interest and possess great wit,
he's concerned with his future and where he will fit.

He hopes in the art world to become a part
in the Hatfield Galleries he's getting a start.
Learning and seeing how pictures are sold
will help him later his career to mold.

To bring an ending to this rhyme
wishing that I had more time
to sum it up in words too few
as I keep reminding Hugh
he can always call me "tu."

Fin

A Dime Is A Dime Is A Dime!
The Saga of Dr. Bob

I know a man whose name is Bob
being a doctor is his job.
While washing his clothes late one night
he had an idea, "out of sight."

Now he was a "penny pincher" from way back
although money he did not lack.
so he thought, I'll save that dime
and I'll save myself the time.
I'll put my clothes in the oven to dry
and at the same time, I'll get high.

Bob and the oven both turned on
and it wasn't before too long,
sipping on a gin and tonic
listening to his quadraphonic
about to take another toke
Bob noticed all the smoke.....

His clothes were black and very burnt
and Bob dismayed his lesson learnt
a dime will always be a dime
but HOW you spend it, is worth the time!

California, Early 1970s

The Levines –
Thank you note

Thanks for our visit, we enjoyed our stay
and your warm hospitality every day
our swim in the pool and sauna too

Peace and Love -
Charlie and Sue.

Miami, October 1975

MKS Esquire

I once worked for a guy named Michael
who had just acquired a motorcycle
not wanting to age and feel odd
it makes him feel really mod!

He has an obsession about the telephone,
he just loves to hear the dialing tone.
In fact he says he would like two or four more,
it gives him a good secure wanted feeling
and in this way he's used to dealing.
He's promised himself to give up smoking
but seems to me he's only joking.

The Tutor Computer was his dream
a colourful, educational machine
for kids to learn on and have some fun
and facilitate the hardest sum.

North in Alaska we had many sales
and Mike returned with incredible tales.
How the people are friendly and warm,
even in the midst of a huge snow storm.

Our "Rep" over there drank to keep going
a pint of vodka each day and more when snowing.
He also worked as a trapper of fur
which in itself caused quite a stir
at the home office here on the coast

of all the Reps. they envied him the most.
He and the guy in the South Pacific,
living in Hawaii he said was terrific.
Demonstrating computers and surfing as well
after passion fruit cocktails, it's easy to sell!

Mike loved to dictate in person not tape
and often would work extremely late,
as in the day it was impossible to write
due to floods of calls, which ceased at night.

As the switchboard closed promptly at five
and that was when Mike would come alive.
He worked into the night and then would dine
on New York steak and a glass of wine.
Sometimes he would return to the piles
of unanswered correspondence and numerous files.

He never seemed able to completely relax
and was always behind in his income tax
from one of the businesses he had at one time
a restaurant, a math game he thought would be fine.

His partner in these ventures was a man named Gene
they encouraged each other and got really keen
on all the latest ways to make some money
some were serious and some were funny.

Dandelion

Divorcees would grab him and flirt with him too
at the least opportunity at any office "do."
Mike was flattered and always in good humour
but was never involved for fear of a rumour.

On business trips he would love to fly
and frequently gave the stewardesses the eye.
He was fascinated by the clubs of the east
the New York night life and enjoyed a feast.

He dreams of having a mad affair
but faced with reality, he wouldn't dare
but if there was someone he just couldn't resist
then he'd be the one to simply insist.
His good looks and fun nature you can't help but like
and sincere honest manner, that's all part of Mike.

Los Angeles, California, mid 1970s

19

The Epic Trek

From Santa Monica, we left the fog
to drive cross country in the "Frog."
A worthy vehicle painted green
the likes of which you've never seen.

After packing, partying and saying goodbye
to friends and neighbours and of course to "Pie."
We finally managed to get on the road,
with knapsacks, ice chest, it was quite a load.

Arizona by nightfall was our first step
to rest and sunbathe and regain our pep.
Meg, a sweet lady was our kind host
she fed us with soup and tuna on toast.

To the land of Enchantment - New Mexico I mean
as to be at the balloon races, we were really keen.
They were multi-coloured and a spectacular sight,
the races started at dawn just when it was light.

We followed by truck, the balloon in the sky
its route in the contest with an attentive eye.
Alas we lost it somewhere unknown
and it could not be contacted by telephone!

So we decided a beer may help us along
and continued our quest singing a song
we felt quite jolly and merry and gay
and quickly early morning turned into day.

Dandelion

Finally we learnt it had returned to the Pad
where it was launched, but we didn't feel sad.
We saw many friends there and had lots of fun
the sky was so blue and we laughed in the sun.

We stayed with Eddy, a friend from before,
a loveable guy you could see more and more.
Also Ginny, an old friend of mine
I'd been meaning to see but never had time.
She now has 2 kids, a house with a pool
which was unheated so the water was cool

We spent some time in old Santa Fe
stayed there overnight and all the next day.
The "Frog" headed East across the great plains
of the huge state of Texas on a road with five lanes.
We slept out that night under the stars
away from the road and the sound of the cars.

We continued to Houston for a day or two
it was more humid but the sky was still blue.
A visit with Pete, Peggy and of course MP
an extraordinary experience, even for me!

The tenants came over early every day
for coffee, to chat, each had their say
and Peggy is wearing a floating gown
as MP leaves for another town.

Actually a suburb, his office is there
after choosing most carefully which suit to wear.
Such a family I've never met
you have to laugh and not get upset.

MP has that Mafia look
no telling what pills Peggy took.
She's crazy and will speak her mind
but a bigger heart you'll never find.

Grandma comes over, she lives nearby
and Peggy swears and gives an obvious sigh.
It's hard in writing to recreate this scene,
but Charlie will tell you what I mean.

Jack invited us up to his poster show
we thought of his camera and decided to go.
They were not exactly what we had in mind
pin up pornography we were to find.
A macrame hanging bed was a treat
you can keep on swinging in your sleep!

From Texas we left for a different scene
to bayou country, wet and green
to Charlie's folk we all did greet
and delicious French Creole food to eat.

In Baton Route we settled in with ease
first to taste the hog's head cheese.
I was bitten by a dog named Pip
and nearly gave Miss Wilma a fit.

Dandelion

She dressed the wound, we drank a beer.
Pip had his shots, no cause for fear,
We ate and tasted every dish
from jumbalaya to fried catfish.

Black eyed peas and grits and gumbo
in the state where all shrimp are jumbo.
The succulent crawfish from the ditch;
I was bitten by mosquitos and began to itch.

Just loved the cracklings, great to munch
as snacks and then we'd have our lunch.
We put on weight down in the South
continually putting something in your mouth.

Into New Orleans Marty flew
and drove to Florida with us, too.
To Pensacola, home of Greg and Gail
they love the Florida life and swim and sail.

Marty's sister I'd never met
she's a tennis pro and plays a set
or two each day, she's very trim
healthy and hearty, tall and slim.

Next day, we left for Jacksonville
as Charlie's sister we had to see still.
Pat and Eric and Shannon too
were pleased to see us come into view.

It was Halloween while we were there
so we had to figure out what to wear

Charlie was a clown with cheeks so red
I was a bat, a poncho over my head
and scarey mask to frighten everyone
to "trick or treat" we had such fun.
Shannon was a gypsy with rings of gold
Eric was a devil looking so bold.

We went to houses in the night
Phyllis was a hunchback and looked a fright.
Pat stayed at home for kids to come
to hand out candy and some gum.

Phyllis arranged our Saturday date
The "Flot" brothers promptly arrived at eight.
To "Driscolls" where there was quite a crowd
and people danced and the music was loud.

We drank tequila and grapefruit mix
the "Flots" stuck to beer to get their kicks.
They loved to dance and had a fling,
they were quite sweet but didn't swing.
Not quite the type we had in mind
but pleasant enough and all Phyllis could find.

Driscoll, the owner set vodka on fire
he was dynamic and never did tire.
Playing the trumpet with all his might
was the definite climax of the night.

Then home to a breakfast of doughnuts homemade
like in the French market, the Flot brothers stayed.
It was delicious and then to our beds
the music and tequila spinning round in our heads.

Dandelion

Pat anxious to demonstrate the powers of his car
took us out in the Blazer, not very far.
Across country, it was a wild ride
as we leapt up and down and got hurled side to side,
Through branches of trees, like a cross country race
then back to their house to drink some more beer
the next day we left, full of good cheer.

The drive to Miami took us a day
munching and driving all of the way.
We finally arrived just after nightfall
and immediately then gave Marty a call.

We looked up a friend that Charlie had known
left a note on his door as he had no phone.
She had travelled with Bob on her trip to the East
and hoped that he hadn't changed in the least.

He was more or less the same as she thought
although had been busted for the hash he had bought.
We stayed with him at his place a day or so
until his landlady told us we had to go.

Then to a house of warmth and music we went
and in the end a month there we spent.
With Alan, Doug, Martha, Jim we had met
and Tania, the psychic, you just can't forget.

The house was a joy, a pleasure to stay
and happiness and love filled every day.
These people merit their very own rhyme
which I wrote in Miami at that same time.

We listened to music and also did yoga
while Alan relaxed, most times in his toga.
Jim swayed in thought and Martha would smile
while Doug played his guitar and sang for a while.

And Tania, as only fruit she did eat
was chopping green coconuts which lay at her feet.
Smells from the kitchen of feasts so divine
of culinary creations we'd serve with some wine.
By candlelight we'd gather all seated around
on pillows round a table low to the ground.

In scarves which floated, we danced at the feast
of the full moon and made exotic food from the East.
Curries and chutneys and yogurt and rice
the food of India, seasoned with spice.

Then on Wednesdays, Tania's classes began
in psychic development to learn that one can
develop the mind in a psychic way
and be more aware in an ordinary day.

More alert and more conscious of just everything
to talk to nature spirits and sometimes to sing.
To feel the energy and let it flow,
to learn and be wise to have strength and grow.
We learnt many things there which will not erase
and will look back often at those happy days.

They were of great quality and will always remain
in our minds and our hearts, always the same.
As lovers and friends we will always remember
our stay at their house in the month of December.

Dandelion

While in Miami, a job on a boat we tried to find
as crew or cooks, we did not mind
what work we did and we wanted to sail
we tried and we tried but to no great avail.

Instead of by sea, we turned to the sky
and winged our way to the Caribbean, having to fly.
It's hard to leave and to say goodbye
and sometimes to wonder the reason why.

But all endings are sad as the cycle begins
besides, we were anxious to put on our fins.
To dive without wet suits in waters so clear
and to lie on white beaches with no care or fear.
As leaving the mainland, we at last did depart
ending our journey, yet a new one to start.

Miami, December 1975

A Poem for Alan

It's hard to fit into your world
expanding yourself to be unfurled.
Like a labyrinth, the way in is hard to find
it turns abruptly in your mind.
Like Knossos, a valley in the hills
of ancient ruins with wonder fills
each spectator in their gaze
plunged into your lifetime maze.
To overcome it's surge and myth
to the sweetness through the pith.
To the centre to the core
it is with greed to demand much more.

To feast yourself on sights you saw
on subtle plains and new dimensions
reaching upward, themselves extensions.
To complement the basic thread
starting and ending in your head.
Through verdant paths that flow like streams
collecting thoughts, creating dreams
opening spaces, some by chance
alleviated in a trance.

Where reality itself is interbred
with rainbow fantasies it has been fed
sprung from past brought up to date
inhaling love, expelling hate.

Dandelion

Demanding truth, yet when it's near
rejecting some, due to a fear
of feeling stripped the few who dare
venture to penetrate your inner being,
extracting the elements used for seeing
into and beyond a point in time,
deep and bottomless, like a mine.

Searching upward with all its might
channeled straight to find the light.
In solitude to think alone
to rotate in silence and to moan.
The way is too narrow yet to share
the pain and feeling of despair
that creeps into your soul like night
silently waiting for the light
of dawn to wake and to arise
the dormant souls and sleepy eyes.
To shine and warm but not to burn
just to illuminate so you can learn
and see the light that glows within
and keep it bright and never dim.
Like a flame may it leap and dart
with love and energy from your heart.

Miami, October 1975

29

Jim

I feel a comfort from your being
and feel a quality you have for seeing
into the depth of the soul where others dare not see
Jim, please always keep in touch with me.

Miami, October 1975

martha

Sweet child, like a flower
may you grow and flourish every hour
and always sing a happy song
I hope to see you before too long.

Miami, October 1975

To, For and About Alan and the Soyburger

Alan is the kind of man
to catch forty winks when he can.
A model baby he must have been,
he loves to sleep, perchance to dream.

When awake, he loves to cook
from his head, not from a book.
The soyburger is his pride
he shapes the patties to be fried.

He's organized and makes up a ton
for the whole household and guests that come.
He makes them fat and wholesome too,
therefore leftovers are but few!

To be eaten, enjoyed and not to waste
he makes them with a delicious taste.
Each one has his personal seal,
which makes them a very pleasant meal.

He's a musician and when playing a tune
captivates everyone in the room.
He has talent in this field
to be exposed and not to shield.

He does whatever he does in a serious way
massage comes first and every day.
He's a serious man, tall and with a beard
a resonant voice, sometimes to be feared.

Dandelion

His authorative nature and paternal concern
make him a target for people to turn.
To seek out comfort and ask his advice
he's pleased to accommodate, without any price.

His compassion and kindness are indeed triple star
and ability to help is way above par.
With glasses he has the "professor" look
especially when intensely reading a book.
Maybe of poetry on yoga or health
on meditation, raw vegetables, materialism and wealth.

His books are serious for the most part
and absorbing information has become quite an art.
I feel he needs influence from a lighter plane
of laughter and dancing and being insane.
To let himself go completely and fly,
to feel the earth and to touch the sky.

After a bath he wears a toga
then to meditate and do some yoga.
Of ginseng root he takes a toke
from a pipe, it's good to smoke.
It clear the channels and stimulate one's sense,
itself is light and not too dense.

Now his beard is shaved and hair not long
and some of his previous image is gone.
He has exposed himself to move
and loses a certain aspect of awe.
This brings him down to a basic level
allowing his jagged edges to bevel.

He feels a downward pull to the ground
with dignity and yet still is profound.
He knows he has a lot to learn
and feels the change begin to turn.
Through yellow rays the pink seeps through
to strengthen, enhance and purify too.

It's great to be kind but good to respond
to the love that is given by those who are fond
of Alan as a person for what he is worth
while he is being and living on earth.

The moral of this story is as follows
with soyburgers you "can't have no hollows."
They must touch the surface and yet rise above
the very personal and filled always with love.
As well as ingredients which balance the season,
mixed in together with "thyme" and reason,
and spice and flavour to taste just right
if this recipe is followed, they'll be out of sight!!

Miami, October 1975

Tania

The Gemini psychic queen
whom I feel I've met somewhere in a dream.
To reconfirm my thoughts and fears,
I know I've known you through the years.
You inspire, create and give me hope
to overcome my "blocks" and cope.
I hope again to see you too
so until that time, I'll say "adieu".

Miami, October 1975

Doug

Like a kaleidoscope, your colours turn
to myriad forms, they begin to burn.
Never will their flames subside
they are eternal, like the tide.
To ebb and flow with vital force
yet leaving fate to take its course.
To melt an experience which will not fog with time
and remind me of you as a cosmic sign.
I feel a unity, a kin to you
and glimpse sometimes you feel it too.

Miami, October 1975

Dèyè Mòn Gen Mòn*

(Beyond the mountains, more mountains: Haitian proverb)

Haiti

Exotic land, Antilles pearl
in crowded streets, the people whirl.
In throngs they walk and carefully thread
and women balance on their head
wares to bargain, sell or eat.
With smiling faces they walk bare feet.
With scarves so bright in brilliant hues,
of magenta, chartreuse, gold and blues.
Earrings that dangle in the sun,
and hips that sway to town they come.

To the market every day
they laugh and chatter on the way.
Past the stands where women cook
and old men grin and tourists look.

The poverty here is so extreme
mixed with wealth beyond a dream.
From the ghettos in the rush
to mansions in the tropic lush.

Hotels surrounded by plants and trees
and gorgeous flowers that smell to please.
The rich, the fortunate who are too few
in a land where hunger is not new.

Behind wrought iron gates the mansions stand
in front of which the beggars hand
is held outstretched in waiting plea
for some small coin to give him glee.

An answer to his starved appeal
assuring him of a simple meal.
The children too will run and beg
and cripples standing on one leg.
All over Haiti you will hear this cry
of give me something - "Ba Mòn Si Bagay!"

It is impossible to give to all
and answer every prayer and call.
Little boys continually flock to your side
asking your nationality and if you want a
guide.
Where are you going and where have you been
do you like Haiti and what have you seen.

Dandelion

Their questions are endless and they always want pay
won't take no for an answer and may be with you all day.
Haitian faces have a beauty deep and rare
unusual, difficult to compare.
Spiced with Creole, once ruled by France
their faces show it in a glance.

Like mahogany, so rich in shades they glow
and warmth and friendliness through them flow.
Of African cult where magic reigns,
and dancing to the distant strains
of taboos throbbing from the hills
where voodoo ceremonies give one chills.

Intoxicated by the drums they dance
their eyes expressed in Voudou trance.
The mystery, like the mountains surround the land
where rich and poor live close at hand.

From the luxury to the grime
it is quite safe, without much crime.
Haiti is not a land for all
but once visited you will recall
her rhythms and contagious smile.

Haiti is like nowhere else you'll find
her vibration is "a state of mind".

Haiti, December 1975

Una Lengua No Es Un Idioma
(Para Carlos)

An understanding beyond a language,
a meaning without a word.
Silent, unspoken truthful thoughts
transmitted by the eyes and mind
which no-one can take and ever possess
or even be aware of.

Its sensitivity is unequaled
and cannot be compared.
This - I have shared with you.
It is not a materialistic gain
but a realm of experience
enriched by people and thoughts.

Through their minds
and their own forms of communication.
Whether it be a different culture from mine or similar,
there is a deeper understanding
which in itself is a presence
to be refreshed and inspired again.

To relate and simply breathe freely
to enjoy a mind and a touch
that's sincere, itself enough.
To feel a bond and not a stranger
even though at times you are one to yourself.

Claude Au Soleil

Ray of the Sun to warm and shine
igniting those who come in touch
with him in any space of time
or who would like to know as much
as they themselves absorb his being.
His strength and all-surrounding force
illuminates the art of seeing
as directness is his very source.

A thought conceived and followed through
projecting as a beam of light.
Straight to the point with no mistake
from cameras focusing centre stage.
Quick to detect the crouching fake
and expose him cruelly to the crowd.
Making him respect and listen to
a voice determined, strong and proud
a solar energy form of you.

for Claude Frioon
Province de Quebec, Canada.
Colombia, South America, Summer 1976

Viva Los Juegos

The juegos stand in bright array
awaiting their first customer of the day.
Exotic liquids from fruits only known
in tropical countries where they are grown.

In lands afar and full of sun
different and delicious every one
Naranja, papaya, guava and lulu
only to mention a few.
Zapote, remolacha, pina, curuba,
tamarindo, mora and maracuya.
Zanahoria, so rich in vitamin A
guanabana, one could drink them all day.

In stands you can select several and blend
of the different flavours there is no end.
Sabrosa y bueno para la salud
thirst quenching and as filling as food.

San Andreas Island, Caribbean, 1976

Viva Los Juegos - song

Remolacha en la noche
la hora de la zanahoria.
Maracuya en la mañana
si - siempre toma lulu.

Desayuno con naranja
y almuerzo con papaya.
Zapote en la tarde
pero - siempre toma lulu.

como no!

Tamarindo guesto mucho
y banana, claro pina.
Si, mora es mi favorita,
sabrosa y solita.
pero - siempre toma lulu
si - siempre toma lulu
y tu
como no!!

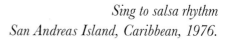

Sing to salsa rhythm
San Andreas Island, Caribbean, 1976.

43

To Judy

Libra Lady, let it flow
enhancing everyone you know
with creative knowledge to learn and share
making first yourself aware.

Let art rise above the mundane pace
where it can breathe in its own space.
Conjure, inspire and thus expand
thoughts expelled by mind through hand.

Networks of patterns of constant change
of myriad shapes of infinite range.
May all turbulence within you cease
to bring a year of balance and peace.

For Judy Heiman
Santa Monica, California, October 1976

To Charlie

As your moons change, may you rise
above the earth toward the skies.
See from within another plane
as one sees sunlight after rain.

Each change brings out another truth
Stopped from blossoming in its youth.
Alive, yet undernourished, not by choice,
until recognized by an inner voice.

Reality instead of dreams
is not always as it seems.
Demanding freedom as its right
Like a plant, it grows toward the light.

Impossible to predict its range
as change itself can turn to change.
As tides turn and ebb and never cease
may each change bring you more joy and more peace.

Santa Monica, California, December 1976

45

To Jim Mally

May the ocean and the sun
fuse into your life as one.
May the rays shine through your heart
Giving energy to your art.
Let your talents outward flow
Exposed to light they soon will grow.
A pleasure to be in your life a while
and be your friend and know your smile.

Santa Monica, California, December 1976

Marty

For the first time a "Ms" she has truly become
she feels a whole person, not half of one.
The time has come to talk of things
of virgins and playboys, to spread her wings.
To fly with the breeze, where it may go
to enjoy just living and letting it flow.

The world is waiting and will always be there
when Marty decides to let down her hair.
From the conventional office which can be a bore
where people are hurrying, trying to score
what they can to become something they're not,
Marty is learning to use what she's got.

She's pretty and witty and hardworking too
but she's not really doing what she wants to do.
Her dream to be able to just simply "be"
her complete self and not to say "we"

She wants to say "I" without feeling pain
to laugh in the sun and to dance in the rain.
To run on the beach, to be on the sand,
to act on pure impulse when nothing is planned.
To have total freedom to think and to feel
individual thoughts, not a cog in a wheel.

To be what she is and after a taste
to follow her instinct and not let it waste.
The time has come herself to find
the thought has been germinating in her mind.
Which path to take, which route to follow,
to think of today and not tomorrow.

Her turmoil, confusion has reached its prime
and will resolve itself with time.
When then at last she can reflect and look
with optimism at her latest book.
She will enjoy her life and glance
and remember when she took this chance.

A turn round a corner in her life
to become a person, not just a wife.
I hope to know you through the years
to laugh with you and dispel your fears
to be your friend when near or far
and always know you as you are.

San Francisco, 1970s

For Mary Scott

To Mary, my dear and beautiful friend,
may healing rays of orange blend
with yellow beams as they transcend
inhaled as prana through the stream.
As pure light expelling from a beam.
Channelled along the paths they find
To heal and strengthen through the mind.
Energy once blocked to now release
Bringing to you your health and peace.

Orange with your vital ray
Yellow sun that lights the day
And brings its brilliance to the soul
To make your mind and body whole.

Om Shanti

Los Angeles, California, February 1977

For Barbara

May orange full with health and vital light
Surround your being day and night
Fusing with power knowledge of the yellow ray
releasing its energy along the way.
To strengthen your body and spirit too
I'll be sending healing rays to you.

Santa Monica, California, May 1977

Sola

To be alone is to know yourself as you are.
I would prefer to be alone than in the company of a
negative thinker.
As people prefer to be loved than to be the lover.
You can lift yourself to any level
and not be limited and suppressed by other people
or their ideals,
because you know yourself as you are
and are not blurred by an illusion.

Santa Monica, California, Summer 1977

To Sam

My life just wouldn't have been the same
without seeing at least one "Dodgers" game.
I enjoyed the crowd with shouts and cheer
the hotdogs, peanuts and the beer.

The guy who with amazing throws
sells peanuts from the ends of rows.
As change is passed along the line
his profit grows and saves his time.

It was entertaining and great fun
especially the score of 7 to 1!!
Many thanks again to you
for an enjoyable evening,

Josh and Sue

for Sam Jaffe (Jackie Jaffe's Dad)
North Hollywood, California, October 1977

Carol

Capricorn Carol, lawyer lady
Venice home, near the sea.
Logic and emotions jiving
always asking "Is this me"?

Surrounded by the Venice people
colourful in rainbow hues.
Driving on the myriad freeways
to downtown her life to fuse.

From the smog to the courtroom
returning to the beach at night.
Changing, loving, hating feeling
which is wrong and which is right.

Slim and lithe and always searching
wondering what will be her fate.
Working, traveling, sports or babies
once again to roller skate.

Freely flying past the ocean
she watches, breathing in the air.
Musicians playing, talking singing
as she wonders, "do they care?"

Meditating on a lifetime
filtering out what matters most

to the peaceful Lake Shrine service
driving there along the coast.

Relaxing in a jin shin treatment,
letting anger and frustration go.
Replaced by new energy channeled in
absorbed as it begins to flow.

She is reborn, recharged with chi
more creative, more aware
still at times she asks the question
even though she hardly dare.

No-one really knows the answer
so the quest will always be
searching for the recognition
to confirm "Yes - this Is Me"!

To me, it is a friend I see
dear, beautiful, sensitive and fun
May she always be herself
and her soul and spirit free.

For Carol Hamilton, on her 31st Birthday
Venice, California, January 8th 1978

For Marcia Stone-Tanck

May the vision of the third eye shine clear
Enlightening your sight throughout the year
As many changes you see in sight
Visualize them through this light.

For Marcia's birthday
Venice, California, 1st January 1978

Thoughts in the Wind

My mind races as the wind
across field and stiles it jumps.
So light and weightless as only air can be,
it races, it gasps, as if to catch its breath.
It is ahead and does not want to wait
to reflect, waiting for others to catch up and contemplate.

It must continue with full rein
nothing must interfere or bar its way.
It is boundless and its limit unknown,
as the wind on its course is blown.
It cannot be hampered by mundane trivia,
it must be allowed to be free and roam
at its own pace and then find a home.

It tugs like a kite escaping the tie
and childishly laughs when it's free in the sky
to fly unrestricted, unbound, without care
heeding to no-one, alone in the air.
It is carried and buffeted and continually plays
twisting and turning in myriad ways.
Enjoying itself in its new found space
not knowing what events next will take place
and influence its future, what pattern to take
it eddies, it whirls and reflects on its wake.

To reflect on yourself, one must look from a height
and in this dimension obtain clearer sight.
The wisdom of learning and simply just being
is the art of thinking and properly seeing.

Dandelion

To not be misguided and not follow through
to allow thoughts to extend that begin within you.

Learning enriches the original thought
wisdom of experiencing is gathered not bought.
So flow where the wind blows enjoying its force
encompass its energy and follow its course.

Santa Monica, California, Spring 1978

To Josh

We share a need
and to need someone is stronger than desire.
It can be fought against and sometimes feared
but at all times respected and revered.

I need you in my life.
I feel a warmth in your presence
and a communication with your soul,
often an endless incomplete feeling
leaving me with a taste for more.
An unknown saturation point
that I have never known before
and want to experience, to taste it to
the ultimate and yet, hesitate.

As circles whose circumferences barely touched at first
are then drawn closer and eventually overlap with time.
So has your life fused and infiltrated mine.
Yet their individual properties that were, after all the magnetic force
which drew them together and united their course.
Feeding their excesses to the other's deficiencies
and in doing so, reinforcing themselves.

To share yourself and enjoy the sharing
to want a warmth that solitude cannot give
to grow within yourself and always caring
for each other as you live.
To know your love is always there
a simple truth for us to share.

California, February 1978

To Josh

You understand me as no other can
to feel what I need and what I am.
To be able to understand and comfort me
is indeed a luxury I can now know
and all sides of my person I can show.

To have this insight I feel is rare
to appreciate, to know and truly share
it is cosmic, it is earth
encompass it and enjoy its worth.

California, March 1978

Helen

May yellow rays surround your being
and open up new ways of seeing
New thoughts and energy channel through
to radiate and heal you.

for Helen Jaffe (Jackie Jaffe's mother)
California, March 1978

Marty – On Leaving

Leaving is mingling old with new,
a fusion of feelings, blending the two.
Decisions, priorities must be worked out,
questions and answers of what life's about.
Can it be captured in just one dimension
be stress free, unbound, relieved of all tension?

The excitement, yet doubt of somewhere unknown,
the adventure, but wondering about being alone
the weather, the trees, the people, the air
all different, all new, all waiting to share
their elements, their energies,
their friendships, their earth
an experience of life, priceless in worth.

It cannot be forgotten, misplaced or lost
thus the pure value of intangible cost.
As a pyramid, the foundation ascends to the peak
built upon levels we consciously seek.

This wealth is stored, used up, replaced
given out, added to, none goes to waste.
Each experience, each outlook only can mean
another new angle from which life can be seen.

Run fast to meet it, yet feel its surge
flow with the changes as within you they merge.
Tides turn with these changes as moon wax and wane
as the body's inconstant but the Spirit the same.

Santa Monica, California, March 1978

On Parting

Time and place brought us together
as they now have drawn us apart.
It is not wise to cling on to the past hopelessly
but rather to let things flow on
Facing truth and learning from its wisdom,
using all experiences to grow and learn
to form the future, which is after all
an accumulation of past and present.

My spirit has been broken, ripped apart and restless too
but in time will heal as it will with you.
My mind is turmoiled, confused and shocked,
my body is exhausted, worn and drained.
An overwhelming sadness fills my heart
that a once close friend is now so far apart.
Our lives once touched - and now again are separate.

Los Angeles, California, November 1978

To Dick Cooper
On His 40th Birthday

A dear friend I'll always know
Wherever in the world I go.
Your Sagittarian fire burns bright
Warming all those in your sight.
Enthuse, inspire and just be there
To comfort, cheer all those who care.

Much love and energy in you I see
May your spirit be forever free.

San Diego, California, December 1978

New Year's Day

As new life begins and old now fades
the past is dimmed, the future bright.
The colours swirl in myriad shades
to fuse yet be in their own light.

So with you, the cycle turns,
taking with it threads just spun.
Using remnants as it leaves
thoughts behind the web it weaves.

All things from different tenses meet
and nothing new is nothing old.
Some are bitter, some are sweet,
but never are they left to mould.
All are used and none remain
in the same form as they came.

Santa Monica, California, 1st January 1979

Dale

Silhouetted in the fog
the notes he played, the time stood still
reached my ears to be recalled
in later years to come at will.

A special time - of year and man
a tune attuned and filled with care.
Harmonizing at its will
fused with mine, a joy to share.

Sharing, caring, loving, daring
to trust a stranger once again.
To touch and understand the needing
as happiness replaces pain.

High energy, it rides supreme
flowing outward from the sun.
Warming days with glowing rays
made our minds and bodies one.

Out of context, but in sight
a reflection that I see.
Mirrored deep as it reveals
silhouetted back to me.

Venice Beach, California, January 1979

Marty Comes to San Francisco

Rabbits bobbing in her garden
calla lilies at her feet.
Wooden gates for those who pardon
passing through her courtyard treat.

Terra cotta staircase leading
to her door of "numero seis."
Strains of Chinese windchimes chiming
owl and lanterns sway and laze.

Red and white checks frame her sight
from the kitchen's back yard view.
Washing hanging out of windows
catching wind and sunshine too.

Across the corner newly painted
is the loo of blue/pink hues
adorned with Laura Ashley curtains
it has to be her "loo of loos".

Cupboard opened out askance
neatly folded sweaters piled.

Dandelion

Temping textures, colours blended
arranged as if they have been filed.

Garage sales delight her now
choosing, expressing herself clearly
one more table to be painted,
an antique lamp, or if not, nearly.

San Francisco living suits her
from the clothes, restaurants and bars.
She settles in with excited fervour
in her eyes, a million stars.

Exploring locally, Polk and Broadway
gays, beatniks, Italian smells.
Yet behind four leafy trees
Marty in her element dwells.

Sandwiched between the Broadway tunnel
and the busy North Beach scene.
Marty in her city setting
is the happiest she has been.

Year of the Rooster
San Francisco, California, 5th April 1981

For Diana Davenport
A Birthday Poem

Pisces lady swimming deep
with your fins instead of feet,
heed to Neptune's powers this year
your ruler of the sea and seer.

See within and sea around
the mystic depths of your playground.
Intuition rules your heart -
follow this and play your part.

Enjoy the changes, with them flow
With no resistance, you will grow.
Peace and love and lots of fun
Enjoy being "thirty-one"!!

San Francisco, California, 13th March 1983

Guy Fawkes Song

Around the bonfire burning bright
see the fireworks in the night.
We all helped to make a "Guy"
whoom goes a rocket in the sky.

Roasting chestnuts, potatoes too,
Joanna, Andrea and Auntie Sue.
Jill and Paolo, Mary and Geoff,
each has a go at being chef.

Catherine wheels that spin around,
Roman candles on the ground
sparklers held in every hand
jumping jacks, watch where they land.

Enjoy our day and Guy Fawkes too
HAPPY BIRTHDAY GRANDPA TO YOU
HAPPY BIRTHDAY GRANDPA TO YOU!

Epsom, Surrey, 5th November 1983

Lyrics: Cox/deVincentiis
Musical Arrangements: Jill deVincentiis
Copyright: Double C Ltd.

Insane at Sainsbury's

The weekly ritual again is here,
secretly, I shed a tear.
Another round of food we need,
a husband and two kids to feed.
The "normal" family of four,
could anybody ask for more!

Frankly, I'd love to live on air,
no meals, no dishes, without a care.
Will I stay awake at night
worrying if my list is right?
Sainsbury's brands are always best,
cheaper, bigger than the rest.

From fresh veg. to frozen meat
a pair of tights - my aching feet.
Is that slimming or makes you fat
"oh no Mum, we don't like that"!

Carts overflowing, what a chore
isn't shopping such a bore.
Picnic lunches, crisps and coke
damn, just when I'd love a smoke!

Dandelion

Let's see what's on special price,
pampers, peas or long grain rice.
Up and down each crowded lane
this habit can become a pain.

No need for any other store
this one has everything and MORE.
The old familiar crowds and queues
Oh, how I wish you had some loos!

For a delivery service I'd gladly pay
oh please Sainsbury's you'd make my day.
I could easily stay at home
with Terry Wogan, I'm not alone.

I could listen to my quadraphonic
sipping on a gin and tonic.
But until that time, I will continue
to shop at your convenient venue.

Please to this suggestion, do take heed
for all the mums like me in need.

Cox/deVincentiis
Epsom, Surrey, England, June 1984

Jackie & Jaci

Sun, sea, beach and sand,
outside dinners, being tanned.
Daily riding on the bike,
in fact, all the things I like.

The paddle tennis, despite the heat,
Mexican food, I love to eat.
The laughs, the fun I shared with you
much love from me, aloha,   Sue

Los Angeles, 14th September 1984

Colin

On his return to New Zealand

It was as if on a bridge we met
passing by, not to forget.
Our paths have crossed and will again
just as sunshine follows rain.

These bridges merely mark the route
of varied paths in one pursuit.
Through the third eye we gain our sight
I wish you always love and light.

Honolulu, Hawaii, December 1984

73

To Pam

As you journey onward to the west coast,
the Aloha spirit you'll miss the most.
May it keep with you, always within,
as one cycle ends, another to begin.

You are going from where I came,
San Francisco, namely Brisbane.
I hope your job brings you much success
and the dollar goes further where things cost less!

Enjoy the fog and the winter chill,
the scarves and hats, I know you will.
The cosy cafes, the music, the art,
Victorian houses, all are a part
of a lovely city by the Bay
where you have now chosen to stay.

The hikes in Marin and Golden Gate Park
the clubs and the theatres after dark.
The workshops, the lectures, the wonderful food
the cable cars, the hills, if you're in the mood.

Enjoy your life as it starts anew
keep in touch, aloha,   Sue.

Alexander Street, Honolulu, Hawaii,
December 1984-January 1985

Malaekahana

O lover of the land and sea
I willed you to come to me.
From the first day with your smile
to walk beside me for awhile.
As with a current, the power is deep,
can almost sweep you off your feet.

Is it we met lifetimes ago
that I feel magnetized, impelled to know
your very core and essence of being,
using the third eye and really seeing.
To wake in your arms is my delight
to feel your warmth throughout the night.
It floods my spirit and my soul
fusing to make our two halves whole.

Malaekahana, Oahu, Hawaii, Spring 1985

Kathy

To Kathy willow floating free,
tall and graceful, like a tree.
Knowing your roots are embedded deep
in the earth beneath your feet.

It is the breeze that makes you sway
gently guiding you on your way.
May your year be filled with light
ever shining, always bright!

for Kathy Feeney, Taurus Lady of Manoa Valley, on her birthday
Honolulu, Hawaii, 29th April 1985

To Larry Dawson
For His Birthday

Aries man with flames of fire,
boundless energy, you do not tire.
Fresh creations always spring
Giving you an endless zing!

You are unique, an old soul too
I am inspired and touched by you.

Honolulu, Hawaii, 5th April 1985

Eve

Rainbow lady may you be
healed and healthy and so be free
of pain and stress and that this weight
will soon be lifted and abate.
Leaving you smiling, full of light
inside and out and ever bright.

May the rainbow's healing ray
fill your spirit every day
written in love, year of the Ox
channelled through your friend - Sue Cox.

for Eve Gate, Rainbow Bodyworks
Honolulu, Hawaii, 23rd July 1985

Vernon

An illusion or a dream,
a reality, which does it seem?
Each merges and can become
separate and yet as one.

The leopard with its spots of black
indicates no turning back.
The past, the pain the hurt you felt
is dimmed and gradually will melt.

Light floods in though you resist
through minute cracks, it will persist
consciousness in us all expands
only through our open hands.
Once glimpsed, it cannot be ignored
acknowledge it, it will reward.

Her wand it beckons calling you
to follow her to fields anew.
Ponder now, what were the odds
your choice, the profound "Queen of Rods".

Be at peace, a state of grace
with heart and mind in the same place
Body, mind and spirt free
the three in one and one in three.

To communicate, express your heart
your feelings and your fears impart
to share yourself and truly give
limitless, you fully live.

Much love and joy and light to you
today and always, aloha.....Sue

51st Birthday poem (Libra)
Honolulu, Hawaii, 12th October 1985

The Three In One and One In Three

Light floods in though we resist
through minute cracks, it will resist
consciousness in us all expands
only through our open hands.
Once glimpsed, it cannot be ignored
acknowledge it, it will reward.

Be at peace, a state of grace
with heart and mind in the same place.
Body, mind and spirit free
the three in one and one in three.

To communicate, express your heart
your feelings and your fears impart.
To share yourself and truly give
limitless you fully live.

Honolulu, Hawaii, 15th October 1985

For Carol Isis

Lovely lady, Aries sun
laugh and dance and sing.
With your gift of music rare
joy to all you bring.

The notes you sound are crystal clear
Directed from the heart
Channelled through you in perfect tone
to finish from the start.

Play your songs forever more
of love and truth and light.
Illuminate those in your path,
reflection always bright.

As you mirror so you change
with tides and time and place.
May you always stay attuned,
the perfect state of grace.

Dandelion

It is my pleasure you to know
at present and in past.
Our spirits join, our hearts our souls
a knot, a bond made fast.

The cosmic egg is opened wide
is cracked from side to side.
The notes you played so long ago,
today they cannot hide.

Their vibrations fill the air
They are inside and out.
Trust them and fully touch yourself
and never more self-doubt.

Lovely lady, Aries sun
Laugh and dance and sing.
With your gift of music rare
Joy to all you bring.

Honolulu, Hawaii, February 1986

Pam Chambers Is A Lady We All Love

She's the star of this evening's famous "roast"
a person to whom I proudly toast.
Her wardrobe is superior,
her complex, not inferior,
Pam Chambers is a lady we all love.

Her hair is short and always free of lice
I've never seen her wear the same thing twice.
Her eyes are big and wide,
her make up carefully applied,
Pam Chambers is a lady we all love.

She's even talked to women in prison
their self-esteem has since then surely risen.
Her next step will be on TV
a female Johnny Carson she could be.
She'll be known across the nation
and create a huge sensation,
Pam Chambers is a lady we all love.

She's taught us all in many different ways
from how to hold the mike - to put on leis.
To speak only with good purpose and be clear,
to overcome the butterflies of fear.

Dandelion

Her speaker's class is time that's well invested,
you'll be stretched and criticized and tested.
Make eye contact with everybody there
just long enough, but not too long to stare.
You'll laugh, be moved, and even sometimes cry,
be frustrated, angry and you'll sigh
"I may never get the hang of all of this"
but when you do - you'll be in perfect bliss!

Speak clearly not t o o s l o w and not too fast,
create an impression that will last.
Dress in a way as to enhance,
this really does much to improve your chance.
Immaculate from her head down to her toes
is the example to us Pam always shows.

With her talent she cannot go far wrong,
and if she does, it's not for very long.
Her motto of "on purpose" guides her way
inspiring others each and every day.
Her smile is most alluring
and she's never ever boring,
Pam Chambers is a lady we all love.

A fellow countryman of mine, she is by birth
making her refined - of sterling worth.
In Oxford where her father was a scholar
an intellect and very much "white collar".
Pam says he spoke with strength

and sometimes at great length.
Like a model, elegant in poise,
she allows herself at times to play with toys,
Pam Chambers is a lady we all love.

Let's give a round, a hearty cheer
for this lady we all hold so dear.
Hooray for Pam, our hearts she's won
with her charm, her wit, her fun.
Recently she changed her name
but her essence will remain the same,
Pam Chambers is a lady we all love.

In case you haven't got it - one more time
Pam Chambers, we think you're "da kine"!!

Written for Pam Chambers
an evening of Winners Circle Star Search
Unity Church, Diamond Head,
Honolulu, Hawaii, 26th February 1986

To Larry Dawson

(author Lawrence Hall Dawson), friend, mentor, philosopher,
writer and above all "a man of the heart".
In anticipation of your book *"The Practical Mystic"*

At last with your wings unfurled,
tell your message to the world.
Brightly burning in the flame,
consumed to be reborn again.
Arise, awake with joy and sing
new lamps for old to you I bring.

To pour new wine in casks of old
is not possible, so one is told.
New containers must be made
for new to shine and old to fade.

The individual strength of everyone
is energized by the rays of sun.
Just as day will turn to night,
so we grow towards the light.

Teacher, your wisdom give to all,
following your inner call.
Clarity herself is clear,
transparent when the truth is near.

This moment draws us ever nigh,
inspiring us to keep us high.
Firey inspiration that you are,
no hesitation to go so far.

An Aloha spirit pioneer,
a kindred soul I hold so dear.
With lightening speed – a shooting star,
just by being who you are.

Recognizer of truth on the earthly plane,
you surely will acknowledge fame.
Truth will always re-emerge
and will be sought with innate urge.

Our reunion this time around
is a commitment to be bound
to fellow souls who think as we,
yearning for truth to set us free.

It is with joy I know you are
always near and never far.
Rare and wondrous you I find
can warm the heart, alert the mind.

In your search to reach the core,
uncovering much, yet always more .
Onward, outward, it has begun
The journey of the "Three in One".

A toast dear friend I give to you,
total support in all you do.
May your heart and spirit be
every joyful, ever free.

Honolulu, Hawaii, 1st February 1986

For Keith Albright of Dallas

Intoxicated by your touch,
the night sped by so fast.
I wish I could make time stand still
and watch the moments last.

The dance, the very pulse of life
continues on by day.
When we stop and think of this
It has to be this way.

The fusion of the yang and yin,
the constant spiral plays.
I felt so light so full of joy,
bathed in a golden haze.

The city lights, the band, the songs
are mixed to blend and mingle.
The warming of your hand in mine
makes all the senses tingle.

Physically we're miles apart
But then you always say

It doesn't seem to matter much
with jet flights twice a day.

It flows and ebbs, and yet
the mind can always take one back,
and the spirit can't forget.

The Aloha spirit never leaves,
the magic's never gone.
Like the delicate pikake lei
the fragrance lingers on.

I felt so carefree in your arms,
the rhythm so divine.
I know it will return again
in a different place and time.

Until that time, I wish for you
much love and joy and light
and memories of happiness
of your "Hawaiian Birthday night".

Honolulu, Hawaii, March 1986

For Sarah George Picot
on her leaving Hawaii

Cancer lady you beguile
those around you with your smile.
Seek the earth where ere you go
to pour your crystal cascade flow.

To nurture, care and sow the seeds,
discriminate the flowers from weeds.
Those that blossom, strong and full
towards the light they feel the pull.

Vibrance, laughter may they be
a part of you I'll always see.
Sister spirit may you be
ever changing, ever free.

Dancing, whirling, twirling spinning,
enthusiastic with each beginning.
New lands, new cities, each different face
beating at their unique pace.

Taste it all and may your savour
each and every special flavour.
Look with wisdom from within to out,
dispelling any fear or doubt.

May you always keep in your course
Reflection from the higher source.
We support the highest and best in each other!

Honolulu, Hawaii, 28 June 1986

The Kamakou Blues (Song)

I've got the Kamakou Blues
and I'm feeling so bad.
I've got the Kamakou Blues
and it makes me so sad.

Well, we took a little trip
and yes, it's over now
and we are all so blue
and let me tell you how.

First there is our leader and his name is Kost
guarantee or refund not to get us lost.
Next I'll introduce to you our own Big Greg
don't offer him one beer when he will drink the keg!

Then there is Big Jim, who is handsome and tall he likes to hike
those mountains and he's been to Nepal.

Dandelion

Cynthia was with us, she knows plants so well,
although there are some species that she just can't tell.
Our guy of the sixties, namely Jim,
and his wife sweet Cindy, and they dance and sing.
Yeah - they are a couple that just loves to swing!

Oriental Allan - has he got some soul,
just don't you tangle with his chopsticks and bowl!
Carol who's in research and was one of the few,
stick around Carol, you'll be "relaxin" too!!

Last but not least we have Sylvie Ann
she makes a mean rum cake in a rounded pan.
As a dessert we all think it's hot
some folks say it's better than smoking pot!

I'm your singer and my name is Sue
and after singing this song, I don't feel so blue
One more time and I'll sing it again
Yeah - the Kamakou Blues can drive you insane!

Kamakou, Molokai, Hawaii, August 1986

93

Halloween Thank You Note to the Chus

Aloha Shirley, Ann and Ming,
enjoyed your lovely Halloween fling.
Trick or Treating in the night
was fun and such a great delight.
Witches, goblins, ghouls and ghosts,
good company and charming hosts.
Delicious food and excellent wine
children's games, a wonderful time.
Once again, mahalo to you
from the "tourist" - namely, Sue

Waikiki, Hawaii, Halloween 1986

To My Friends –

Year of the Rabbit - 1987

You are the dear ones who support me in light.
You are the mirrors reflecting my sight.
The gift of a friendship cannot be compared,
a treasure to cherish, a love to be shared.

As I grow in my life, you have all played a part
and have been at my side through every new start.
Mahalo, I thank you, please never lose touch
I miss you and love you all very much.

May this coming year be a memorable one
abounding in joy, success and more fun!

Honolulu, Hawaii, New Year's 1987

Massage

Sore muscles
sore feet
Go for a treat

After a day hike,
a trip on your bike.
A swim in a race
a jog at a pace.
Massage hits the spot
works out that knot.
Relax your tired feet
give your body a treat!

Relax, rejuvenate, refresh with Massage therapy.

Honolulu, Hawaii, 1989

Curt – My Friend, Lover and Sharer of the Flame

The love of the ocean we both know and share,
her moods and her changes of tide.
As waves are separate yet part of the whole
so to you I have opened my heart.

Love comes from the source
to which we all long to return.
To seek within to unite,
becoming whole feels right.

I feel the pulse long afterwards,
but I can recall it anytime
as the truth will always last.
It does not tarnish over time,
it cannot be corrected.
It always stands alone and proud
and never is neglected.

Once recognized one must go on,
the path becoming clear.
Take caution to relax the grip
and clutch too much from fear.

One must go on and in joy and peace,
it seems so clear and bright and new.
The tighter we hold on, the faster it slips through,
like the fine grains of sand.

I feel myself sinking and falling falling, like a falling star
The comfort, the caring it brings back to me
so there I want to remain.

To expand ourselves
and for the seed to grow that we have sown
like the sea with its waves, your love washed over me
and the sound and touch
resonated afterwards throughout my whole being.

I surrendered myself to the ocean,
to taste the salty tang and sharpened air.
So your waves washed over me
and the more I surrender, the
freer I became
till finally I gave my heart and body and soul
to mingle and become as one.
It is not a light and easy thing,
but deep and meaningful within.

The fear of being swept up
and then dashed aside on the rocks
or gathered up in harmonious movement
to rise and swell together.

The sea with its eternal tide,
her moods, her depth, her blue.
The turbulence in times of storm
the calm and peace - all true.
True to herself and
not heeding to the distractions of others.
In touch with the power and so to overcome all fears.

Dandelion

The constant movement, always change,
never stagnant, or completely still
it is so with you.

I surrender to the truth
and this is something one must know.
As the moon reflects upon the earth
with her lunar silvery glow.
So we reflect on those we love
and ourselves more fully know.

The joy of giving love to you
watch the circle that love again reflects as we learn.
We face ourselves and cannot lie,
the truth will always win.
A lover is a friend, an art
with added lines to play a part

Better friends that last than lovers brief
but can the two be one?
To laugh, have fun and sleep beside
to share their joy and grief.

I crave this oneness in myself
and long for this to share.
To learn and grow much wiser too
through love and constant care for you.

Your hazel eyes so kind and deep,
your smile just goes to show
that warmth and strength well from within,
I recognize and know.

From where it is I know this face
this touch, caress and kiss.
From lifetimes past I can recall
rare moments of this bliss.

To stand alone we know we must
together and yet apart.
True love it does not smother one
but flows right from the heart.

I recognized your soul reach out
to reunite once more.
The flames ignite as they inspire
breathing from their core.

Surrender to the power of love
its essence so divine.
For it can bring you riches rare
a feeling so sublime.

The more we look inward, the deeper we see
broadening our vision, that is the key.
To see much further, the pane must be clear
to widen our vision - dissolve all the fear.

Honolulu, Hawaii 1989

Steve

A truly special man you are
reaching toward your highest star.
Each day as I connect with you,
each day, I know you more.
How much sweeter is the fruit
when nearer to the core.

Let go of all things in the past
the power is only now.
Follow your inner spirit guides
and they will show you how.

Our ideas blend, we set them free
into the waiting world.
Til clear channels we become
new directions will be unfurled.

To create, inspire a work of art
must come from deep within.
An opening of the mind and heart
all humanity can win.

Once I saw you as my friend
to walk beside you on the road.
Our paths have crossed, our lives have touched
the seeds have now been sowed.

Sue Savill Lucas

I feel the unique essence of you
the palm trees sway beneath the stars.
The grass of night is wet with dew
a moment in time we shared was ours.

A time where old fades out and new prevails
as history is made.
Go forward with your brightest light
into the new decade!

for Steven Tedrahn, for the New Year
Kailua, Hawaii, January 1990

For Eleni Armeniades

Panther Grecian goddess you
in jungle island bliss.
The wildness in your spirit is
enhanced when lovers kiss.

The soft wind blows where'ere she goes,
the coconut palms are swaying.
You'll feel her essence as she sings
her guitar softly playing.

Feline being touch our hearts,
bring your joy and laughter.
Your humble healing and loving power
is wisely well sought after.

Primal colours that you wear
their brilliance never daunts,
or overshadows the inner light
which unconsciously she flaunts.

From distant lands you've traveled far,
your spirit free to roam.
Now has alighted for a span
in your Hawaiian island home.

Her Aloha spirit charmed you here
to learn from higher planes.

To meditate and heal your soul
amid the tropic rains.

Kahuna gods and ancient myths,
your memory stirs again.
Awaken to those thoughts and return
to rid yourself of pain.

Love is by far the strongest force,
it cancels out our fear.
Illuminates the path we tread
and keeps us on our course.

In past lives we have been
in healing temples which rise
above the mists on sun parched earth
against the azure skies.

It is no fate our paths have crossed,
once more we have our link.
Each time is stronger than the last
more powerful than we think.

A kindred soul to share and play
the same tune, the dance of life.
A weaver in the tapestry
a seeker of the way.

Quicksilver sister with your proud mane
stalking on the beach.
Remember that which we have to learn
is always what we teach.

Dandelion

Grow and flourish in these isles
quench your thirst awhile.
Cheating dreams and living them
in your own artistic style.

May your visions all become
a reality for you.
Enjoy each day and live your dreams
as only you can do!

Kailua, Hawaii, 7 July 1990

For Bob's 52nd Birthday

A reflection that I see
mirrors back from you to me.
Happiness and joy, fill my heart
To grow together, not apart.

A time for patience to heal the hurt,
to pick the flowers that lay in dirt.
With hearts open to this flow,
only then we truly grow.

You hoped and dreamed and then you knew
My feelings were the same for you.
To recognize we feel the same
The wild unicorn becomes quite tame.

We talk of essences and time
And even as we do,
we listen as there are no words
for us to channel through.

Dandelion

If it's pure water that we seek
We must expel all fear.
Draw from the wells of lifetimes past
to make the present clear.

Drink from this cup again my love,
refill your thirst once more.
Return to your natural source
a connection with your core.

Our cups are filled, our lives entwined,
we know it feels right.
As long as we respect the truth
and lean towards the light.

It's said that timing is the key,
That accidents are none.
It feels special with you close
our spirits merge as one.

Kailua, Hawaii , 17 September 1990

Avalon

A simple cottage on the lake
with your low key-shaped door.
Candlelight with gentle glow
lapping water, canoes that moor.

Peaceful sunrise, moonrise too,
mountains strong and serene.
Villages nestled at your feet,
frangipani smelling sweet.

Through the archway, inner space
your doors open within.
Starting with the spirit free
looking outward to just be.

My time was stilled to spend with you
inside your walls and yet,
a freedom and a peace of mind
that I will not forget.

Relaxing, reading, walking, loving
breathing in the mountain air,
To be in perfect harmony
to rest without a care.

Refreshing water of the lake
cleanses my spirit too .
A time with my thoughts, a special time
to know my lover true.

Thank you, Terima Kasih
Lake Batur, Bali, Indonesia, 6 October 1990

To Bob On Valentine's Day

Dearest Bob, my sweetest love
welcome home to me.
I missed your presence every day
in your arms I'd rather be.

We come together once again
the memories stir inside
of when we played and laughed with joy
a friend in whom I can confide.

Lovers of the soul unite
together we burn a brighter light.
Twin flames of the single heart
can feel each other miles apart.

Our deepest thoughts, the way we feel,
entwined but yet so free,
to express ourselves and live our dreams
apart, but yet a part of me.

To feel your needs, your hopes and fears,
to grow together through the years.
Acknowledge this true love divine
accept it, my "special" Valentine.

Kailua, Hawaii, 14 February 1991

Virgo Bob

Bob, a man of Virgo sun
mercurial mind that ticks
with percentages and computer runs
how do you get your kicks?

Let go of structure, be as free
as tigers roaming wild.
Dance all night and sleep all day
awaken your inner child.

Be spontaneous, without care
and everything will flow
into place and be alright,
as you reap, you'll sow.

Fantasies of windows wide
open to the night.
Alluring lovers surprising you
holding you so tight.

Dandelion

Your senses heighten and your mind
never stops to think
of logic, dollars, how to save,
at the point you sink
into the arms of sleep and dreams,
nothing stays the same.

The players change, the soul expands
as it plays a bigger game.
As your partner and future wife
I complement you too.
Acknowledge your essence, support your goals
I love you, always, Sue.

Kailua, Hawaii, 17 May 1992

For Teresa Barker

I know your heart is broken,
let go of pain and fear.
Breathe out the past, breathe in the new,
a brand new dawn is here.

Let in the healing light
and feel it fill each cell.
Illuminate each speck of dark,
its rays will make you well.

Surround yourself with friends who care
communicating from the heart.
We all help each other on the path
each plays a very unique part.

A thread in the tapestry of life
is woven every day.
Each step we take however small
propels us on our way.

Dandelion

Healing comes from deep within
channeled from our source.
Open yourself to the stream of life
and flow along its course.

Reality was once a dream,
a vision seen so far away.
Awaken to your inner child
she longs to laugh and play.

Light brings a brilliance to your soul
to make your mind and body whole.
Energy once blocked to now release
bringing you an inner peace.

- Namasté -

Year of the Rooster
Kailua, Hawaii, 9th February 1993

Donna

Trade winds blow and you must go
to a state where mountains are capped with snow.
Sparkling lights and starry nights,
the city's pulsating beat.
Casinos, shows and slot machines,
the chilly nights, the blazing heat.

Once caressed by her gentle touch,
Hawaii can steal your heart.
Implanted in your memories
from which we cannot part.

The waving palms bid you farewell,
the ocean breezes too.
The islands bathed in light and sun
and all your friends and all the fun.

The Aloha spirit never leaves
the magic's never gone,
like the delicate pikaki lei
its fragrance lingers on.

for Donna Hopkins
on leaving Hawaii for Las Vegas
Kailua, Hawaii, 14 March 1993

Farewell to Teresa

You are the ocean, you are the sea
No Ka Oi Hawaii.
As you leave her sandy shore
you'll sigh and you'll inhale her more.

As you pull yourself apart,
Hawaii will always be in your heart.
Her gentle winds, her swaying palms
wave to you with open arms.

Your friends are here
their love is dear
No Ka Oi Hawaii.

As you leave your island home
to a destiny unknown,
you'll know you always will reside
with her Aloha spirit deep inside.

for Teresa Barker
on leaving Hawaii for Oregon
Kailua Beach, Hawaii, 26 April 1993

Valima

Sparkling eyes, clear and blue
mirrors to your soul, the inner you.
Your heart is open and your mind
the perfect partner you will find.

It is no chance our paths have crossed
always seeking, never lost.
Flow with the magic sounds you hear
feel the "aina" become the seer.

Reach high and yet anchored to the ground
nourish the feminine you have found.
Her seductive island charms
trade winds blowing, swaying palms.

Soothing waters wash away
cares and worries of the day.
Forbidden fruit calls out to us just within our grasp
dare we try it, dare we ask.

Electric current through each vein
it is recharged and returns again.
So different we are and yet the same.

Each one of us is but a link
a thread, uniquely woven, covered by ink.
The sameness and the oneness shows
core rooted in earth, the spirit knows.

Light pulls us upward to the skies,
the circle born, it burns, it dies.

Dandelion

Eternal the flame, ignited passion of fire,
truth supreme rules and will inspire
creative thoughts which always need
nurturing dreams on which to feed.

The ocean's strong and gentle power
feel her surge and swell.
Each wave never fails to break
just how we cannot tell.

The dawning of awareness draws
us inward by karmic laws.
Once we have truly seen
we cannot be as we have been.

Renewed, refreshed as we ascend
experiencing every curve and bend.

The paths all vary to the Source
everyone has their special course
May you always walk in light
and love illuminate your sight.

Vailima, Samoa,
March 1997

Hawaii No Ka Oi

Hawaiian music fills my home
windchimes sound on the lanai
trade winds and gentle rain
I know that I am home again

My love affair with the islands is never over
the white beaches and turquoise water
welcome me back

My friends surround me and my telephone rings
my life continues yet is never the same
as it was before any experience.

Dandelion

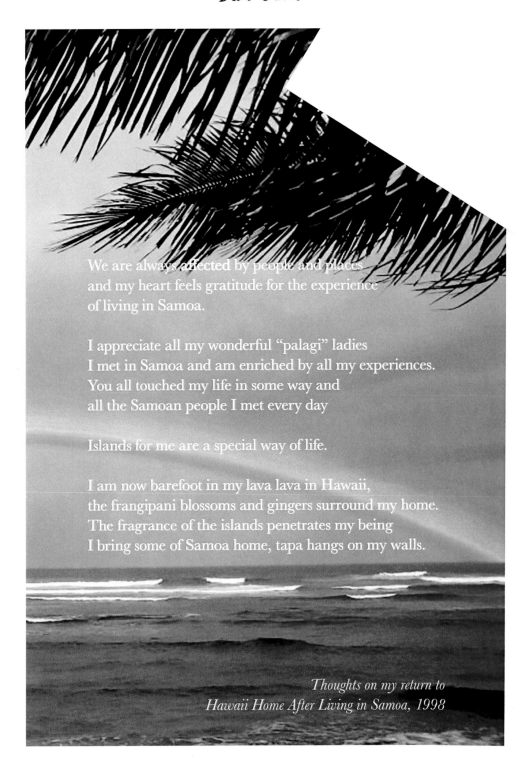

We are always affected by people and places
and my heart feels gratitude for the experience
of living in Samoa.

I appreciate all my wonderful "palagi" ladies
I met in Samoa and am enriched by all my experiences.
You all touched my life in some way and
all the Samoan people I met every day

Islands for me are a special way of life.

I am now barefoot in my lava lava in Hawaii,
the frangipani blossoms and gingers surround my home.
The fragrance of the islands penetrates my being
I bring some of Samoa home, tapa hangs on my walls.

Thoughts on my return to
Hawaii Home After Living in Samoa, 1998

Mary Cox (our mother)

The golden leaves, the changing trees,
our Autumn days are here.
Caring, loving all our lives
we have always known.
Now it comes full circle
and our turn has begun.

We may not know your inner thoughts
love doesn't need to know.
You were always in our lives
watching us continuing to grow.
Giving us a stable home, even after leaving,
now it is with heavy hearts that we begin our grieving.

We will always hold you close
always see your smile.
Grateful for your being
in our lives a while.

We will never fill the space
that you have left behind.
We will remember all the good
sweet, gentle and so kind.

As we scatter in the ground
those ashes that remain
we know in our hearts and minds
our lives will never be the same.

Dandelion

Love lives on in the heart
the spirit's free, at peace.
We'll know you in a different form
and never will we be apart.

for the memorial to our mother
Norwich, England, November 1998

For Joanna de Vincentiis

I send you love, I send you light.
Keep your spirit strong.
Peace and joy be in your heart
Focus on the right, not wrong.

Things aren't always as they seem,
and clouds can block our view.
But behind these clouds, the sky is blue,
and life begins anew.

Always keep your channel clear
open to receive
anything you really want,
create and then believe.

Learn from the challenge which is life
Fight for what you know.
Be true to yourself, no matter what
And let the energy flow.

Stepping stones come in your path
To help you on your way.

Dandelion

Use them wisely, know their power,
learn something every day.

Be grateful for all the good
Be thankful for every friend.
Your family and all you love
from beginning to the end.

Heal your heart, your very soul
Be a firey light.
Illuminate all those who touch your path
and give them clearer sight.

Love is the greatest force by far
More priceless than all gold.
A commodity and yet itself
cannot be bought or sold.

Make every day a special one
Fill it with magic and fun.
Remember, even though there're clouds
Somewhere, there's always sun!

Written for my niece in Portland, Oregon
and Bakersfield, California, January 1999

For Bob, My Husband

Where has my true love gone?
Are you in my dreams?
Do you ride the nightly skies?
Love's not always what it seems.

Unleash your spirit, set it free!
Let your love fly back to me.
Drench me with your kisses once more -
don't turn away and close the door.

My heart follows where you go
connected to the cosmic flow.
Let us soar to greater heights
have warmer days and closer nights.

Are you still within my reach,
to touch my hand and soul?

Dandelion

This partnership without you is half,
I need you to make it whole.

Search inside and find again
the passion to rekindle.
Ignite the flames and feel the glow
before it begins to dwindle.

I recommit to us as one,
as the New year comes around,
let us begin to build again
and fall back on sold ground.

I wish for you all happiness
and health in every way.
As love, the greatest force on earth
fills each waking day.

Bakersfield, California, January 1999

Bob at 62

The sweetness of your night time kiss
permeates my day.
As if your spirit's reaching out
and yearns for me to stay
in your life, beside you now
and in your future life.
A realization from within
you want me as your wife.

Our paths have crossed so many times
and with each twist and turn,
we merge, we separate, change and yet
we always seek to learn.

The spaces between the bars
where sunlight filters in.
The darkness where the growth takes place
the anger and the pain.
All the hurt, the suffering
to return to home again.

Dandelion

Life comes around full circle
complete and without fetter.
We come to know ourselves
and each other better.

Take this day, your special time
to savour every touch.
For every journey from the heart
expands our souls so much.

Seek only for the highest good
in everything you do.
Be wise and happy every day
and to yourself be true.

I wish you the best in your life always.

for Bob on his 62nd birthday
Turtle Bay, Hawaii, 17 September 2000

Ann

Wishing you a year of tennis,
your spinning shots are quite a menace.
We love to have you at Turtle Bay
in our group, you inspire our play.
It gives us a challenge and lots of fun
I'd really love it if I won!

It's always a pleasure.

for Ann Hatter on her birthday.
Turtle Bay, Hawaii, 2000

For Chiara Grimaldi

Red haired woman in a whirl,
Autumn leaves around you swirl.
Russets, amber of forest hue
compliments another you.

Underneath the ocean tone
To Neptune's waters, free to roam.
Creative spirit wells from within,
her music, song soars on a wing.

Singing, dancing is her right,
then she comes alive at night.
Reach to your depths as there you'll find
The harmony and peace of mind.

Keep in balance and touch the ground
Only earth has a certain sound.
A primal base on which to pound.
To shape our fantasies and schemes,
Pisceans feel and create their dreams.

Secret wishes, we do not see
often are the hidden key.
Intuitive, playful, but a deeper wish
Slips through your fingers like a fish.
Grasp your wisdom, hold it near
And manifest your dreams THIS YEAR!

on her birthday
Hawaii, 27 February 2001

In Remembrance of Gerry

To know someone, one does not forget,
their imprint is on the soul.
It stays forever, keeps us young,
strong and always whole.

It is at times of sadness, we stop and see the light,
draw inward to our inner selves
to give us clearer sight.

The energy of life pulsates us still
toward the ONE where all paths lead, yet myriad turns they take.
We are all one and still unique
as the ocean and the wake.

It brushes us and then moves on
to the invisible beyond.
If we could glimpse into eternity and taste her scented breath
would we live on earth in bliss in sweet serenity?

At each ending, life begins in different shapes and forms
for all our knowledge, we cannot know
unless we ourselves are blessed.
Can peace of mind set us free, free from worldly worry
free to be and free to dance, the spirit knows no hurry.

We can only live our lives on earth until we die,
completely full, completely spent and leave behind the cry.

Dandelion

When our human form and spirit merge into the great Divine
the oneness we all will come to know in which there is no time.

I send my love and hold you dear
as in my heart I know,
though physically we are apart
our spirits never go.

*written on the death of Gerry Dawson
and sent to Larry Dawson in Portland, Oregon.
Turtle Bay, Hawaii, February 2001*

On the Brink

We spend our lives teetering at the brink
pondering on being, while we think.
Ironic is this, for the opposite is true
not thinking, but feeling the real you.

Open your heart, your mind and soul,
doing this will make us whole.
Find out what's important and what we crave
for we cannot take papers to the grave.

Hold on to life, savour each touch,
each moment in time can mean so much.
When we choose to be alone,
a luxury, but when it's thrown
upon us, when there is no choice
we flounder and struggle with our inner voice.

I know my poems are inside
and need another place to reside
I send my love, my hugs to you
aloha no, your soul friend, Sue

(part of an email letter to Larry Dawson)
North Shore Oahu, Hawaii, 1 June 2001

Barbara Towle On Her Birthday

Teacher, surfer, North Shore wahine,
tall and slender in her bikini.
At home she contemplates the sea,
how big are the waves really going to be.

She grabs a board, she's on her way
paddling out to start the day.
A bike ride up Pupukea hill,
she's on the move to get her fill
of exercise, fresh air and always fun
enjoy the run - a downhill run!

Dark beer is her favourite drink
sunsets on the lanai, a time to think.
Grateful for her island home
even though she likes to roam.

Exploring Portugal, France and Spain
traveling on trains, you're not the same.
Experiences change us inside out,
we grow and expand, without a doubt.

Integrate both sights and sound,
ethereal sky and solid ground.
To learn another's way of life
appreciate their daily strife.

Move on through life and cherish friends
regardless of the current trends.
Our wishes today and through the years
Many Happy Birthday Cheers!

North Shore, Oahu, Hawaii, 26th July 2003

On Love and Oneness

The tapestry of life is woven all the time,
each piece unique, essential, be it coarse or fine.
Appreciate the differences, but know we are the same,
born of a spiritual source, returning there again.

The weft and warp, as on a loom,
make intricate patterns and the moon
illuminates us on our way,
sunbeams warm our path by day.
So much greater is the whole by far
as is the galaxy to a single star.

Each thread contributes to the whole
expanding every heart and soul.
Although, often from our source we're torn,
where love prevails, we are reborn.

Each breath is new, a pranic move,
it heals, it nourishes and is used to soothe.
Where love exists,no one one is apart,
the world is one energy and one heart.

Pupukea, Hawaii, 25 October 2004

134

Farewell to Christina

In a condo, by the ocean
on an island in the sea,
lives a lady and her husband,
the one and only, Edward G.

(chorus) Oh Christina, oh Christina
We will all be in the soup
When you up and leave us standing
All your friends in the spiritual group.

They decided bright one morning
That they would leave our sunny shore
And move over to the mainland
Where less can buy you more!

(chorus) Oh Christina, oh Christina
We will all be in the soup
When you up and leave us standing
All your friends in the spiritual group.

Ed will miss his trails and mountains
Waterfalls and island hikes.
Perhaps though on the mainland
You will invest in mountain bikes!!

To the mainland, to the mainland, to the mainland, off they go
We all wish you much aloha and hope you both avoid the snow

You will miss our island beauty
And our ocean of sparkling blue.
The group will of course continue
but we'll all be missing you!

From the east coast to the west coast
And then to these lovely isles.
All the flying, all the packing
But all the frequent flyer miles!!

(chorus) Oh Christina, oh Christina
We will all be in the soup
When you up and leave us standing
All your friends in the spiritual group.

Did I pack it, did I toss it, perhaps we agreed to send
All the parcels and decisions, enough to drive one 'round
the "Bend"!!

Yes, we'll miss you oh so much
but we know we'll keep in touch,
by the phone or by our emails
or in person, if all else fails!!

To the Mainland....

As we know, we're all connected
and in our hearts, we all are one.
Many blessings on your journey
Great adventures, lots of fun!!

(chorus) Oh Christina....

Copyright: Roosters Ltd.
March 2005
Melody: "Oh My Darling Clementine
New Lyrics: Sue Savill Lucas
Guitar: David Mosley

Farewell to Ina (Aina)

There's something about being around Ina,
there's something very special, we know, we know.
There's something about being around Ina
That makes all our hearts aglow.

In our group, she has really been a part
always speaking to us from her heart.
We know for Hawaii you'll be yearning
So will look forward to you soon returning!

There's something......(chorus)

Here's a little summary about our group
Just to keep everybody in the loop...

Alan is like many grown up boys,
he's very happy just playing with his toys.
His idea of an evening quite divine
is soaking in his hot tub drinking wine.

Hostess, Kathy always open and so fair
After all, she was once a famous Mayor.
Politics and real estate interest her today,
she grew up living in the Unity way.

Christina with her very detailed eye
Keeps us all on track as time can really fly.
She likes nature and going on a daily walk,
swimming in the ocean and interactive talk.

Then there is a lady named Sandy
Knowing her can really be quite handy.
Knowing where your moon is and what's in the stars,
are you from Venus or possibly from Mars?

David, her husband can play the didgeridoo,
another fellow rooster and an Aquarian too.
He used to have a ponytail but since he's got rid of that
He's a very peaceful man who likes to stroke the cat.

Marvellous Marvalyn is very good at sharing
She adds her views to the group and is always caring.
If you want a fairy godmother, we can grant your wish
And introduce you to our magical " Lady Trish".

A guy who we have all grown to like
That's our wicked, wacky Mike.
Many interests in his unique style
loves tennis and coffee and has a nice smile.

Last but not least, the poetress, me,
I always feel at home in the sea.
Perhaps I'm a mermaid who came ashore
traveling the world to learn a lot more.

There's something... *(chorus)*

Tune to "Someone's in the Kitchen with Dinah"

New Lyrics: Sue Savill Lucas
Guitar: David Mosley
Copyright: Roosters Ltd.

Larry Moves to the Pearl

I know you've been in quite a whirl
getting re-located in the "Pearl".
The many houses you have know
big or small, they're always home.

Enjoy the walks and Babe will too,
the ambience, cafes, another view.
Another thread of life you weave,
now is the present, the past you leave.

I look forward to seeing you
as every day unfolds anew.
As always you are in my heart
even when we are apart.

Much love I want to send to you
stay in the flow, aloha,   Sue

for Larry Dawson on his move to Pearl District
Portland, Oregon, 2 August 2007

For Janet Murphey

All life is a mirror reflecting in the light,
see your dreams and treasure those always in your sight.
Your family is near at hand, your friends each have their smile.
It has been a pleasure to be in your life awhile.

Peace of mind will set us free
From worldly cares and strife.
It is then the spirit dances
in the circle that is life.

Our soul merges with the Great Divine
A oneness in which there is no time.
I send you my love and hold you dear
as though physically we are apart
Our spirits never go.

Kahuku, Hawaii, 5 May 2008

Lynn

The veil of life and death are the same,
we all return from whence we came.
Our hopes and wishes for today,
our light, our shining star.
Let your light be bright,
your tears in the night
be shed for those who know
not only are we infinite, but never cease to grow.

We mourn our loves of many lives
until we are joined once more.
What now is done begins again
and spirals from our core.

We know that love comes from the heart
and love can never die.
Even though we always ask
the obvious question "why".

Trust in Spirit and release
and all our fears will ever cease.

for Marvalyn Heery, on the death of her son Brian
Portland, Oregon, 29 December 2008

Appreciation Poem
for Barbara Simmons

So many things, but where to start,
you always come from an open heart.
I remember the many things you would bake
Especially the wonderful Valentine cake!

You were such a supportive role
in "Solos" Hawaii Singles Club
whether doing a workshop or in a pub,
It just wouldn't have been the same
if you hadn't joined in our game.

Never judging what others do,
those kind of people are all too few.
You always have a kind word to say
and many times have saved the day.

Your positive outlook and love of life
keeps you in the flow.
A helping hand you freely lend
Always willing to help a friend.

Much aloha and love to you
All of the above, I appreciate..
Sue

Honokaa, Big Island, February 2009

Dandelion

Cassie

Even though you are apart
the Aloha spirit keeps in your heart.
May you remember her azure sea
from lush Windward to arid Lee.
The mountains and the magical rainbow
stays with you wherever you go.

The swaying palms wave you farewell,
the trade winds soothe the soul.
The perfume of flowers linger on
long after the actual lei is gone.
The island beauty and her joy
we all say "Hawaii no ka oi"!!

Her wand it beckons you
to follow her to fields anew.
Embrace the new but cherish the past
friends on the path will always last.

it's been a pleasure to share with you
parts of our lives, aloha......Sue

for Cassie Young, on leaving Hawaii for Arizona
Hawaii, 31 May 2009

Who Am I?

I am spirit
I am human
I am woman and sometimes man.
I see myself as different,
individual and others can
at times glimpse into the inner me
for moments and stay awhile.
It is in these times of linking that we go the extra mile.

We seek the truth as students of our lives and more
as into many entries there's always one more door.
I am but a thread in the loom of the great experience of life
On an earthly plane, a sister, a lover and a wife.

All we need is love so all the songs keep saying,
but in the stillness of the mind, we are all one soul in praying.

I am a traveler seeking still
as around the world I go.
Striving to always do my part of keeping in the flow.
The tapestry we all can weave,
the treasures we all share.
Authentic self comes shining through
and this is when we care.

To thine own self be true
is well known, but do we heed.
As in nature, a mighty tree
can begin with just one seed.

Plant the seeds and reap the crop
Growing inward to the top.
Laugh a lot and have much fun
body, mind and spirit one.

Hawaii, June 2009

Illusions

Are we chasing an illusion?
Running from our dreams?
Sages say throughout the ages
life is not always as it seems.

A cascading veil obscures our view
of what lies beyond our sight.
Beads of dew of rainbow hue
A kaleidoscope of lights.

Aqua waters near the shore,
navy blue in the deep.
Immersed among the whitecap waves
Awakened from our sleep.

Water in all its myriad forms
washes over you,
becoming one with the bigger sea
in many shades of blue.

Is illusion then fantasy or fact?
Are dreams are what is true?
We ourselves are only right
when we surrender and become the light.

We bring all things into that beam
so that they transform and see
where inner stillness does reside
that's where we will truly be.

To be alive, aware, awake we touch
the inner peace we all deserve
and which we all want so much.

That light transcends our every thought
our every move and care.
We study, read and meditate
And say a simple prayer.

People are one as we all know,
with nature as our guide,
we follow on the path and then
 will have freedom at our side

Are dreams then what is true
and life is but a dream?
Catch the light, live in its ray,
bring all things into its beam.

We will never be alone and never have to fear.
The truth will set us free.
The light already is within
We only need to "see".

Kailua Beach, Hawaii, May 2010

Jason and His Juliette

You met at the bewitching midnight hour,
you felt its pull and power.
Twenty-one years ago on this day
you joined each mind and heart,
embraced every change and every move as each has played a part.

The freedom to be yourselves - this has been your creed.
If love is there, our hearts are free and this is all you need.
Many years have passed since then and oceans have been crossed,
but love when nurtured and allowed to grow is never ever lost.

Enjoy this special day as refreshing rains give you
a chance to rest, enjoy the peace and start each day anew.
It's my pleasure to be in your lives if only for a while
To know your family and be your friend
and know each other's smile.

Turtle bay, Kahuku, 10 December 2010

Farewell to Wyn and Don

What can one say of Wyn?
She's English and aims to stay trim.
She likes to eat each day by six
Which sometimes gets her in a fix.

She has a passionate love of sheep,
her cell phone even has a "bleat"
She's a good listener and in a trice
from her social work background can give good advice

Don tends to look arty and debonair
even with his receding hair.
He also is a computer whiz,
but rarely you'll see him "in a tiz."

Even though he's now retired
he's still very much admired.
He doesn't take the time to snooze,
thinking of an upcoming cruise.

Malaekahana nights and days
they have spent, a chance to laze,
Don has a very creative bent
especially when camping in a tent.

They'll miss their pool and jacuzzi tub.
We'll miss them in the British Club.
Members for so many years
we're all sure to shed some tears.
An adventure only expands the mind

Dandelion

Remember "shaka bra" and "da kine"!
Island sushi, mahi and poi
the colourful pools full of koi.

Slack key guitar and island ways
Airport greetings with beautiful leis
Her waving palms bid you farewell
Hawaii has a certain spell.

We've hiked, we've barbecued and so much more,
who knows what else is still in store?
We will all be anxious to hear
Their new experiences this coming year.

Remember the famous wild boar hike
Don wouldn't attempt that one on a bike!
We forded a river at the very start,
clutching ropes and wading, quite an art!

"It'll be just a path," Wyn tells us all,
luckily nobody took a fall.
Paul and Elizabeth were covered in mud.
At least there wasn't the odd flash flood!

First visitors to our Portland abode
adapting to public transportation mode.
They loved exploring the city, the Triple Falls hike,
Silver Falls and going by bike.
A jazz concert in the park,
picnic lunch, we stayed till dark.

Birthday and holidays we've been happy to share
With Wyn and Don – a delightful pair!
Even though they're going away,
we know they're in our lives to stay!

Obviously one could go on and on…
with many memories of Wyn and Don.
I have picked out but just a few -
I hope this is enough for you!

They say a change is as good as a rest,
Wyn and Don will put that to the test.
Just a jump across the pond
to visit London of which Wyn is fond.

They love the opera, theatre and art,
I'm sure New York will play its part.
The famous Broadway shows,
Fifth Avenue shops with elegant clothes

A different tempo, a different beat,
a different time zone, a different heat.
I'm sure the 2 months in New York will go by fast
especially if you have a blast.
Perhaps New York state will go out on a limb
and simply rename their town "Brookwyn"!!

A toast, dear friends, we give to you,
may your hearts and spirits be
ever joyful, ever free.
The Aloha spirit never ends.
The magic's never gone.
Like the delicate pikaki lei,
her fragrance lingers on.

Malaekahana Beach/Turtle Bay, Hawaii, 11 - 14-May 2011

Poem for Dan Lucas

Dear Dan you left us way too soon
I met you on your honeymoon
on Oahu, in Hawaii nei
where one is greeted with a lei.

We really enjoyed our Bakersfield stay
inner tubing down the Kern river on a hot summer's day.
Just the perfect place to be
I nearly got tangled up in a tree!

In Portland, great jazz in the "Pearl"
fun exploring somewhere new.
The Paddle Steamer with a "Gorge-ous" view.
Another excursion we had a wonderful time
in the Oregon vineyards, tasting wine.

We send our love as we all grieve
although our spirits never leave.
Though physically we are apart
you will live on in every heart.

Turtle Bay, Hawaii, 20 May 2011

Poem for Trish

Bathe in the beams of this super moon,
illuminate your soul.
Surround yourself with love and light
for you are always whole.

Peace of mind will set us free
from worldly cares and strife.
It is then the spirit dances
in the circle that is life.

Where love exists no-one is apart,
the world is one energy and one heart.
The power of love is always there
even when we no longer care.

It knows no bounds and soaring high
we ride up on her wings.
To help us heal, forgive and where
the unleashed spirit sings.

It has been my pleasure to walk with you
to share our hearts and prayer.
Know that all those who surround you now
are those who really care.

Behind every cloud is a rainbow
after every rain is the sun,
from the darkness of night to the brightness of day
we know in our hearts we are one.

Summer Solstice, Kahuku, Hawaii, 21 June 2013

Poem for Bill Chung

As you open to the sky
and ask to know the reason why.
Breathe in the light and healing rays
as love transcends our waking days.

Know all those around you and who care
will align themselves as one,
so together the harmony for which we long
builds up and makes each of us strong.

This strength is shared among us all
and can be used if one should fall.
It picks us up and carries us through
to heal and create a healthy you.

Learn from each other and it seems
we support our own and each other's dreams.

Visualizing we know has power
draw on this at every hour.

We know we all have this within,
it is ours to freely take.
As a drop of water by itself is small
but many make a lake.

Love we know is a mighty force
and cannot be denied.
Focus on this for both pain and disease
will shrink and step aside.

Sending you my very best
thoughts and loving rays.
May you heal inside and out
in these golden Autumn days.

Portland, Oregon, 1 November 2013

For Myrna Zezza

Treasure all the time you spent
for our earthly time is merely lent.
One never knows the ebb and flow
of nature's tides from which we grow.

We can only give in to the surge
surrender to the current.
Even when our time on earth is finished
our shining light is not diminished.

The soul at last is free to roam
and return to its true spiritual home.
An indelible imprint is left behind,
an external comfort is ours to find.

Be grateful for having loved
a truly special man.
You will always feel the bond
as only Soulmates can.

When connected to another's soul
we feel a complimented whole.

It's hard to be the one who's left behind
our joining is now a different kind.

The love of two hearts held as one
entwined joy, the pain, the fun.
An indestructible bond is formed
all these elements now are mourned.

All this joy, the sorrow and the pain
once transcended is not the same.
Be in nature every day, breathe in her healing rays,
draw from her wisdom and her truth in all your coming days.

Focus on love which surrounds you now
the present is where we are.
No-one can take the time away
you shared with Bill so far.

Memories are kept alive
are precious as is gold.
All aspects of our life will change
and a new path will unfold.

Be at peace, you are not apart
Bill is always in your heart!

Portland, Oregon, November 2013

For Alan

Unity of Portland book circle
"The Untethered Soul"

A strong belief is at your core
and always leaves you wanting more.
Soft spoken, gentle and always kind
this book, the group have stretched your mind.

Excess baggage has got to go,
enjoy the ride, go with the flow.
Be free of limitations now
follow your path, the way of Tao.

It has been my pleasure to share with you
in our circle of light, Aloha, Sue.

Portland, Oregon, 18 November 2015

For Barbara
Unity of Portland book circle
"The Untethered Soul"

Affirming to meditate every day
to focus and help you on your way.
Observing those around you with new sight
as you gain more clarity in this light.

Release old patterns, breathe in the new
transforming to a radiant you.
It has been my pleasure to share with you
in our circle of light, Aloha, Sue

Portland, Oregon, 18 November 2015

For Donna
Unity of Portland book circle
"The Untethered Soul"

From a joyless but lovely home,
stifled and nowhere else to roam.
You felt trapped for far too long
like a caged bird without a song.

Now you can spread your wings and freedom taste,
fully living, there's no time to waste.
You are quieting the chatter in your head,
each moment now you are present instead.

Let go of anything you do not need
and the goodness of change will take its lead.
It has been my pleasure to share with you
in our circle of light, Aloha, Sue.

Portland, Oregon, 18 November 2015

Sue Savill Lucas

For Mark

Unity of Portland book circle
"The Untethered Soul"

You give your energy every day
to patients old and new.
Now it's time to focus inward and on you.

Your photographic eye can see beyond the surface to the core.
You have shared a lot in our circle group but left us wanting more.
It has been my pleasure to share with you
this book, our thoughts and dreams.
To learn reality is rarely what it seems.

Each path has a different route, but they really are the same,
leading back towards the light, the place from which we came.
It's possible to be in a state of "constant play"
alive and fit in every way.
More changes are surely yet to come,
for we know, change is never done
Go with the flow, it's just more fun!

Portland, Oregon, 18 November 2015

For Merle

Unity of Portland book circle
"The Untethered Soul"

Many changes for you in the last 7 years
learning to trust without the fears.
You are committed to a spiritual way
the "Tao" for you is here to stay.

If problems arise you can quickly turn
to solutions from which we all can learn.
Happiness is accepted for you Merle
as an oyster hides an illustrious pearl.

It has been my pleasure to share with you
in our circle of light, Aloha, Sue

Portland, Oregon, 18 November 2015

For Norma

Unity of Portland book circle
"The Untethered Soul"

You are entrenched in nature and Mother Earth
isolation will loosen it's tightened girth.
An eagle "Aumakua"* is for you
soaring higher to get a better view.

It lifted you out of the mundane
and since then you have never been the same.
It was a very powerful sight
circling you with conscious light.

Share your gifts with those around
from the infinite sky to solid ground.
It has been my pleasure to share with you
in our circle of light, Aloha, Sue

*Aumakua: Hawaiian. In mythology, an aumakua is
a family god; often a deified ancestor; protector*

Portland, Oregon, 18 November 2015

For Paula Mantel

Paula is an angel
she walks on sacred ground,
because although being a Taurus,
she's down to earth, I've found.

She's an awesome teacher, inspiring every child
and has the clever knack of taming the wildest one to mild.
Her subbing is renowned, schools all want her to stay
but Paula prefers to simply live each and every day.
Enjoying her freedom to come and go
she's intent on "being in the flow".

If your memory is failing, Paula can help you there,
her classes are amazing and the price is fair.
Another class with quite a wide appeal
is "Reading Power", paced to make one reel!
Learn this skill, absorb a lot,
retain the facts, it's really "hot".

Housesitting in all kinds of places,
Paula's integrity enhances and graces
every home she visits or stays
in a myriad different little ways.
She often leaves her host a gift
her presence is always to uplift.

Originally she hails from the Midwest
but Hawaii's the home she loves the best.

Her soothing trades and aqua sea,
walking the beach, she'd rather be.

Important to her is family time
as caretaker and mentor she plays a role.
Sometimes though this can take its toll.
She knows the importance of time alone
and how inner work can set the tone.

A trip to India, carefully planned
to gain wisdom from this ancient land.
Meditation to her is the key
as through the third eye we really see.

The Hunger Project played a big part
in her life, and still is dear to her heart.
After Chernobyl, to Russia she went
helping children heal from this horrific event.

Her eyes are bright and clear
she always brings good cheer.
When she needs some time alone
she curls up in her lair.
Cozy and contented,
she's just being "Paula Bear".

Dear Paula, you are a unique friend,
without judgement, a helping hand to lend.
We always seem to keep in touch,
sharing our journey, means so much.

Portland, Oregon, March 2016

Kindred Souls

Kindred souls to share and play
the same tune, the dance of life.
Weavers in the tapestry,
seekers of the way.

May our visions all become
a reality for us.
Enjoy each day and live your dreams
knowing that we are "enough".

Portland, Oregon, October 2016

167

About the Poet

Originally from Norwich, England, Sue has been writing poems for several decades. She has lived in Hawaii on the island of Oahu for over 30 years. Sue now divides her time between Oahu, Hawaii, and Portland, Oregon with her husband, Bob Lucas, enjoying two very contrasting lifestyles.

Made in the USA
San Bernardino, CA
07 May 2018